Auto Accident Injury In Houston?

How an Attorney May Help Pay Your Medical Bills
And Get You Compensated For Your Injuries

By Ryan B. Bormaster, Esq.

ISBN: 978-1-941645-01-7

Design and Published by:

Speakeasy Marketing, Inc.
73-03 Bell Blvd #10
Oakland Gardens, NY 11364
(888) 225-8594

www.SpeakeasyMarketingInc.com

DISCLAIMER

This publication is intended to be informational only. No legal advice is being given, and no attorney-client relationship is intended to be created by reading this material. If you are facing legal issues, whether criminal or civil, seek professional legal counsel to get your questions answered.

R.B. BORMASTER & ASSOCIATES, P.C.

2425 Fountain View
Ste 290
Houston, TX 77057
(713) 714-4000

www.BormasterLaw.com

TABLE OF CONTENTS

ATTORNEY INTRODUCTION

Ryan B. Bormaster was born and raised in Houston, Texas. His practice includes Personal Injury Law including but not limited to Trucking Accidents and Automobile Accidents. He also practices in the areas of Criminal Defense, DWI, Real Estate Law and General Trial Law. He has successfully prosecuted and defended trial cases and civil appeals and has been fortunate to gain a wide variety of experiences to draw upon when needed.

Mr. Bormaster prides himself on his work ethic. He is committed to his clients and their cases and is dedicated to core values such as honesty, integrity, hard work and open communication. He has been known to accept representation of those in need on a pro-bono basis as he truly believes that one's ability, or lack thereof, to afford a high priced lawyer should not dictate whether they are deserving of quality representation from a lawyer that cares. When it comes to you and your case, he is always available and if he cannot answer your legal question he is sure to know who can.

He is admitted to practice law before the Supreme Court of Texas and the United States District Courts for the Southern and Eastern Districts of Texas. He is or has been a member of the State Bar of Texas; the Texas Trial Lawyers Association; the Harris County Criminal Lawyers Association; the Houston Bar Association; and the American Bar Association.

He grew up in Houston, Texas where he graduated from Bellaire Senior High School. He went on to receive his B.A. in Government with a minor in Philosophy from the University of Texas at Austin. He then attended Texas Southern University's Thurgood Marshall School of Law where he graduated Cum Laude with his Juris Doctor (J.D.).

An Overview of AutoAccident/Personal Injury Law

Interviewer: Why are auto accidents an area of law that you cover? What is it about it that you like? What do you figure you help people with by being in it?

Ryan Bormaster: I've always prided myself on the David-versus-Goliath approach. I believe in victims' rights. I believe in consumer rights. I believe in standing up for the little guy. Any time an automobile accident takes place – assuming the other driver has insurance – it's David versus Goliath. You are the individual; you're the little guy, and the insurance company is the billion-dollar pocket.

It doesn't matter that Allstate says you're in good hands; it doesn't matter that Travelers invites you to come under the umbrella. No matter what the insurance company tells you, in my opinion, their job is to pay as little as possible. They're going to look for every which way to pay out as little as possible in most circumstances.

Big Corporate Interests and Big Insurance have made large strides in Texas through tort reform. There hasn't been a consumer-friendly judge on an appellate court in the last 20 years. All of the appellate decisions bear that out. They have whittled away at the rights of the little guy. Even our governor down here has expressed that his job – his goal – is to get lawyers and plaintiffs out of the courtroom, because lawsuits are "bad for business." That doesn't do a whole lot for you when you're hurt.

They've passed things like "loser pays" under tort reform. All that does is empower big companies to hire giant law firms with enough lawyers to paper the little guy so much that they inadvertently miss something and lose on a technicality. Even though they're really injured because of someone else's conduct, now for the pleasure of that injury, they're paying the bad guy's lawyer fees.

Interviewer: That's terrible. I didn't realize it's gotten like that.

Ryan Bormaster: Yeah, it's horrible. They have passed things like damage caps, which basically is a message to the jury that you're not intelligent enough to hear the facts of this case, review the evidence, and decide for yourself not only if someone's done bad, but if they've wronged someone else and how much that is worth. That's taken away from the jury now. The juries don't even know that, because they still render their verdicts, and then the judges reform them down.

You end up in a situation where a jury renders a verdict, the judge then thanks the jury for their time and excuses them, reforms that judgment down, and we the taxpayer end up paying for things like Medicare, Medicaid, and that kind of stuff. On top of that, I'm not even allowed to say the word "insurance" in a courtroom anymore.

I had a case not too long ago where my client had a compound fracture. She had bone sticking out of her arm. A jury sent in a question to the judge and asked the judge what percentage, if any, was paid by insurance. Because of the tort reform laws, judges aren't allowed to talk about that. The judge couldn't answer their question. The jury awarded zero in past medical, and gave my client $5,000 in pain and suffering.

When I approached them afterwards and asked, "Why zero?" they came back and they said, "We didn't want her to double dip. "No explanation. I wasn't allowed to explain to them that insurance companies have a right of subrogation; they take every penny before the plaintiff gets a dime. I got to tell them afterwards that, because of their verdict, the insurance company got all the money, and the victim got zero, and they were mad.

They've passed these laws because of lobbyists for big business and insurance companies. This is the result, in the real world, for victims here in Texas. They've recently passed a law that says I'm not allowed to show medical bills anymore. I'm only allowed to show that portion that has either been actually paid, or actually incurred. The conservative big business judges at our esteemed Supreme Court—one that are elected because of big business and big insurance, have gone on to say that just because it comes as a bill, doesn't mean it's actually incurred. There could be a contract or right of reduction such as Medicare, Medicaid, or insurance and so all you are allowed to present are those lower amounts.

Juries used to look at medical bills as a function of determining what money to pay someone for pain and suffering. One hundred thousand dollars'

worth of medical bills means that guy got hurt, versus $10,000, which is what you get for a visit to the emergency room today.

They have no real measuring stick anymore, because we're not allowed to show the bills. It's just been whittled away, whittled away, whittled away. The same judges keep getting re-elected thanks to these lobbies. Organizations like the Chamber of Commerce, who form satellite organizations like Citizens Against Lawsuit Abuse and Citizens for Tort Reform to make them sound like grassroots organizations to fool voters into believing they're supporting good causes, when in essence all they're doing is lining the pockets of big business and big insurance at the expense of the victim. I chose this area of law to be a voice and an advocate for those victims.

Interviewer: If someone's been injured, is there hope? Is there even a point in trying to get money from the insurance company, or should they just give up?

Ryan Bormaster: No, they should never give up. There is always hope. So long as there's a breath in lawyers like me, there is a chance to level that playing field in the courtroom. Although they have tied our hands and they have made things very, very difficult, people still take up that challenge. People like me and the lawyers in my firm who fight the good fight every single day for the victims are just becoming more and more creative in how we make those arguments so that we can level that playing field and try to overcome some of the burdens and hurdles that have been placed before us.

AUTO ACCIDENT SCENARIOS

Interviewer: What kinds of vehicles are associated with accidents that you could help people with? Is it just cars, or what other kinds of vehicles?

Ryan Bormaster: I specialize in trucking accidents – 18-wheelers versus passenger cars. I handle every type of case and every type of automobile accident case imaginable, from low-impact soft tissue damage cases to broken bones and surgical cases to death cases.

If you've been in any kind of automobile accident my firm can help.

Interviewer: Cars, trucks, motorcycles, RVs – everything, right?

Ryan Bormaster: Everything.

No-Fault in Texas

Interviewer: I've heard about fault and no-fault states. What does that mean, and what's the law in Texas?

Ryan Bormaster: Actually, that's a good point. I'm glad you asked me that, because I'm only licensed in Texas. The advice or the explanations that I give related to these kinds of topics are limited to Texas law. If someone's reading this book and they live in a different state, it's very important that they check with a lawyer in that jurisdiction. I can't tell them for sure that their state's law is the same as Texas'.

In Texas, no-fault is basically personal injury protection or med pay. Those are two categories of insurance that people have the right to purchase when they purchase their own liability insurance on their vehicle. They can add personal injury protection and/or med pay. Basically what that means is, regardless of fault (it doesn't matter if they were the cause of the accident, or someone else is), those policy provisions require that person's insurance company to pay out to the limit of whatever they have there for their recovery.

In Texas, the average is $5,000 to $10,000 in personal injury protection. If you were out on the road and you caused an accident, even if it was your fault – like you rear-ended the guy in front of you – you can file a claim with your own insurance company, and they're going to pay your medical bills up to $10,000 if you had $10,000 in PIP, and/or your lost wages at 80 percent, typically.

If you missed a week of work, and you normally would get paid $1,000 a week, they'll pay up to $800 of that. They'll typically pay 80 percent of your lost wages, and 100 percent of your medical bills – up to that limit.

Interviewer: If you're in a collision, then – let's say the police ticket you and say it was your fault, or it just comes out that it apparently was your fault – your case isn't doomed. You can still get compensation, right?

Ryan Bormaster: First off, just because the police report suggests that an accident is your fault does not mean it actually is your fault. Most officers are not sufficiently trained to render that opinion and most accident reports are not even allowed into evidence except in a redacted form to demonstrate the date, time and people involved. Always get the advice of a lawyer. As far as PIP and Medpay go, you can get compensation if you've got med pay or personal injury protection. There's a difference between the two. PIP will allow you to take personal compensation. Med pay is limited to the medical providers. It does not compensate for your lost wages, and the insurance company will issue a check directly to those providers in most instances. PIP, by far, is the superior choice. PIP allows you to recover for your medical and your lost wages, and they'll write that check to you, and then you can go negotiate with your doctors.

Interviewer: What if I am in an accident and the other person's insurance company is calling me because they believe I was at fault? Is my case doomed?

Ryan Bormaster: Immediately contact your own insurance agent. Assuming you have liability insurance, your own agent will be able to get a claim filed with your insurance company to handle the other driver and his or her lawyer. That's why you have insurance. It's there to protect you in situations just like that.

Additionally, you should contact or consult your own personal injury lawyer immediately. Often times, the accident may not be your fault, but the other driver has hired a lawyer to try to flip things on you. A good attorney will be able to help you to navigate that, and hopefully ultimately turn things around on the other driver and recover for you. Note that your own insurance company will defend you, but they will never try to recover for you. Only your personal lawyer will do that for you.

COMMON MISCONCEPTIONS

Interviewer: What have you found to be people's top three misconceptions about auto accidents? Maybe because they watch too much TV, or they don't know; what things do you hear over and over and over that they're telling you but are wrong?

Ryan Bormaster: I hear, "I'm going to get at least three times my medical bills." I hear, "With a lawyer, things are going to move faster." I hear, "Tort reform means they're going to pay me more, because there are no more frivolous lawsuits." Those are the three things that I typically hear.

"I'm going to get at least three times my medical bills." Not anymore. That was the heyday of personal injury law. That was more than 20 years ago, before the insurance lobby and big business took the lady at McDonald's that spilled coffee on herself, and spun it into tort reform. Most people don't know about that lady. She suffered such severe burns – from her breasts all the way around her crotch area – that she had to have skin grafts. She had to have round-the-clock care. She couldn't dress herself. She couldn't bathe herself. That coffee was at a rolling boil, melting through the Styrofoam, when it was handed to her. McDonald's had had hundreds of prior complaints, but refused to change their holding temperature.

The jury verdict was only the profits from one day's coffee sales – one day's. You don't hear about any of that, because that's not sensational enough. That doesn't sell papers. Instead, you saw on *Seinfeld* and *The Tonight Show* and all over the country the brilliant marketing minds of big business and the insurance lobby turning that into "lady spills coffee, gets a million dollars."

Interviewer: I guess I'm ashamed to admit that I thought they should put her on a dunking stool and dunk her into a vat of boiling coffee for doing that. Now I hear these facts.

Ryan Bormaster: Most people don't know. Because of the great marketing and the spin put on tragedies like her's, for true victims the days of three times the medical bills are long gone. This generation has grown up seeing billboards that say, "Been injured on the job? Call such-and-such. I'll put this much money in your pocket." They are desensitized to the plight of real victims. They think that it's all a big scam, and that lawyers and doctors and tow truck drivers are all in cahoots together, pulling a scam.

We start off behind the eight ball trying to overcome these misconceptions. It's unfortunate, but it used to be that they would do that as a multiplier. Today, you're lucky if you get your medical bills and your lost wages plus a few thousand dollars. I hearken back to the example of the lady that had her bone sticking out of her arm. All they said that was worth was $5,000.

CLIENT CONCERNS & MISTAKES

Interviewer: What are the top three concerns people have about what's happened to them?

Ryan Bormaster: Their first concern, inevitably, is "What's going to happen with my car?" if it hasn't already been addressed. Their second concern is, "How much

am I going to get paid?" The third might be, "What if there's not enough money to cover my medical bills?" Also up there – it might be tied for one, two or three – is, "I can't stop working even though I'm hurt because I've got to pay my bills at home. Is that going to hurt my case?"

Interviewer: Do you have any answer to these top three concerns?

Ryan Bormaster: Sure. First of all, if you're not at fault, the other driver has insurance, and your property was damaged, then you're going to get some money. Under the law in Texas, you're only entitled to what it would cost to put you back into a similar vehicle in the condition it was in immediately before the accident.

It doesn't matter that you owe $10,000 and your car is only worth $4,000. If that's the case, you're only going to get $4,000. The contract that you signed when you purchased that vehicle, between you and the car dealer, and the separate contract between you and the lender, meant that the lender paid that purchase price already. You owe them that money because they loaned it to you, regardless of the value of your car.

Texas does permit Insurance Companies to offer other types of insurance, like loan/lease payoff, or gap insurance, which should cover the difference between the value of your vehicle and what's left on the note. While your vehicle is being repaired (you're entitled to choose your own repair shop), the other driver, if they're responsible, is required to put you in a loaner vehicle. Those things you shouldn't be concerned with. A good lawyer will be able to make that happen for you very quickly.

As far as going to the doctor, because of tort reform, and because of the way things are set up in Texas, your medical bills and your treatment and your physical condition have to be believable to a jury. The jury is going to hear the other side say to them, "What would a reasonable person do? What would a reasonably prudent person do if they were really injured? Wouldn't they be getting treatment to feel better? He just wants you to believe the only reason he worked was to pay his bills. He could have taken time off to go to the doctor. He couldn't do the job if he was so hurt that he couldn't work; besides, his employer wouldn't have let him come to work."

These are the types of arguments that I'm going to hear in a courtroom, and you're not doing yourself

any favors by not addressing your true medical concerns. If you're not really hurt, then there's no reason to go to a doctor. If you are, there's no reason not to. As a matter of fact, you'll make things worse if you don't.

Interviewer: Do you see people wait too long? How long is too long to see a doctor?

Ryan Bormaster: You do not want a gap. You need to be going in the ambulance to the hospital. Don't worry about the bill. A lawyer will take care of those things with you and will address them properly. You need to be going in the ambulance to the hospital immediately from the accident.

The reason for that is because that way, there is a baseline. You've got a medical report. You have told the doctors at the hospital what happened, what you are feeling and what condition you are in. They have documented it immediately after that accident. Then, you need to be going in to see your own primary care doctor, or some doctor, as soon as possible thereafter – within a day or two. You went home from the hospital, you tried to take care of yourself; maybe you used a heating pad or an ice pack, maybe you took over-the-counter Tylenol or Advil, and things are stiff and they're now getting worse. You need to keep that documentation going.

If you leave a gap of days in between, the other side is going to be able to say, "Wonder what happened during those days in between?"

Interviewer: Essentially, they're going to twist it and say, "You weren't hurt, obviously because you waited."

Ryan Bormaster: Correct. They're going to say, "You didn't start feeling hurt until you got a lawyer. Isn't that right? Then all of a sudden, you had all these other doctors."

Interviewer: What are some things that people unintentionally do that makes their case harder to win, or reduces the amount they'll get, or ruins their ability to get compensation?

Ryan Bormaster: The number one thing they do is they aren't consistent with their treatment. They get comfortable. They're not following their doctors' orders. As a part of that is they're not telling their doctors about their complete medical history. I can't tell you how many times they think, "If I don't tell the doctor, nobody's ever going to know that I was injured ten years ago. I really don't want that coming up here, so I'm just not going to tell them."

I promise you the other side will find your claims history and your history of doctor's visits. There is a computer record out there that most if not all of the big insurance companies have access to and can run what's called a "clue report" on you. They can type in your information, and it'll generate any time a claim for anything has been made to an insurance company that's a member. They can figure out where you've lived and where you've worked. They're going to ask for the last five to ten years of work history. They're going to investigate whether or not you've ever gone to the hospital, whether or not you've missed time from work because of an injury, and so on and so forth.

A good lawyer is going to dot their "I's", cross their "T's", and do their job. If you have not told your doctor everything, they're going to twist it. It's not going to be, "I just didn't think about it at the time." It's going to be, "You lied to your doctor. Why should the jury believe anything you have to say?"

Interviewer: It's terrible.

Ryan Bormaster: That's right, but that's what happens. That is a big thing that people do, unintentionally, that can destroy the value in their case. Another thing they do is they don't cooperate with their lawyer or the insurance company. If your lawyer's office is calling you, it's to check up on you and it's because they need to have contact with you. It's to make sure that you're doing everything you can, and to update you on the status of what your lawyer is doing. When you're not cooperating, or you're not showing up to therapy or you're missing appointments – that will harm your case.

Finally, social media: that's a huge, huge no-no. I guarantee you – because I have access – there are ways that lawyers can get on Facebook, MySpace, Twitter, LinkedIn. Anything and everything that you can possibly think of that's out there, they can find it. When you are walking into your deposition or answering to the insurance company in a recorded statement and telling them about how awful you feel, and there's a picture of you the night before dancing on a bar, that harms your case. You have got to make sure that while you're going through this, you are not killing your case by posting pictures that are from before the accident or trying to keep up appearances on social media in the wrong way.

It's one thing if you're talking about, "I feel awful today." It's another thing if you're talking about, "It's my birthday. I'm going to get my drink on." You don't want to do that while you're going through this. It leaves the impression that you are not as injured as you say you are, because truly injured people aren't going, "Woohoo!" on Facebook. They're sitting at home going, "I don't even want to get on Facebook right now. How do I get better?"

Interviewer: What do you tell people if they're being barraged with calls from the other party's insurance company saying, "You've got to give us a statement"? Do they have to? What should they do?

Ryan Bormaster: If you do not give them a statement, you are not going to ever get your case settled. It is highly unlikely. The insurance company has a duty to its shareholders, and to its policy holders, to only pay claims it can independently corroborate. They have got to do their own investigation. Absent a recorded statement, which is a very valuable tool, they can say, "This guy doesn't care that much. He must not really be that hurt. He's not cooperating with me."

You also have to remember this: at the end of the day, the adjustor – although they work for the enemy, big insurance – is still a person. They're a human being. They put their pants on one leg at a time. They go home, they kiss their husband or their wife, they sit around the dinner table and they talk about their day. If you rub them the wrong way that can change the way they input things into the computer system. When they input things into the computer system one way or another, that human factor can affect the value of your case.

Even though you feel wronged and even though it's not your fault that you're in this situation, you have to be cognizant of the human being on the other side of the phone because they're a human being and they have feelings. You could take your frustration out on them inadvertently, and they could take that one way or the other. How do you know how they're going to feel on a particular day at a particular time? You don't know that person's quirks. You don't know what they find humorous and what they don't. You don't want to risk the value of your case by rubbing them the wrong way.

I will also say this: it is always better not to give that recorded statement until you've got a lawyer. Your lawyer can better prepare you for that recorded statement, can be on the line with you when you give it, and can even ask questions of their own if they don't like some of the answers you gave.

Human beings think that they're negotiating and making a deal, and they're being smooth or they're being impatient or they're being like, "Gosh, you should know this. You do this every day. What are you wasting my time for?" Those things come out in that recording. Those feelings come out in that recording. You don't want to be in a situation where later on, a jury is listening to you and they're listening to that recording, and you sound unsure of yourself, or you are trying to remember and you just can't, so it appears like you're making it up as you go.

If you hit your head and you can't remember, or you blacked out, don't make it up. That's horrible. The other side will see through it, and so will the jury, and they will go to town on that. Go see a lawyer. Get a consult. Have them whisper in your ear and help you through that recorded statement, because that is going to be what sets the tone for the liability and damage aspects of your case going forward.

Do Insurance Companies Act as an Alternative to Attorneys?

Interviewer: Does someone really even need an attorney if they're in an accident? Won't insurance just handle everything and cover everything?

Ryan Bormaster: You absolutely need an attorney if you're in an accident. There are a lot of different reasons why.

What you have to remember is, any time you're dealing with an insurance company – whether it's your own insurance company or the other driver's – the goal of the adjustor is to pay as little as possible to resolve your claim. Most of the time, you're never going to get what the true value of your injuries and damages are without legal help.

Personal injury lawyers are trained in this area. They have experience dealing with adjustors and insurance companies, and they do it every single day. Just like you probably have a job that you do every day, and are hopefully very good at it, you know first-hand that it's rare when someone else can just walk in and do your job to your caliber.

Lawyers are no different. They specialize in an area and work on it day in and day out, and are likely to bring a huge value to your particular set of circumstances. I'm also going to give you an aside. Most insurance companies run algorithms in order to determine a value of the claim. What they do is they'll put up spreadsheets. It varies by insurance company, but they're very similar in the industry.

Basically what they'll do is they'll have categories. They'll say, "What type of injuries?" and they'll put them in a category. They'll say, "What's the amount of the medical bills?" and they'll put them in a category. They'll say, "What's the jurisdiction? "They don't mean Texas; they mean county. The reason they ask that is if the accident took place in one county, it may be a more liberal set of voters making up that jury pool than in other counties.

Harris County, for example, is very conservative. That means that the odds of a breakout judgment or runaway jury are much lower than in a county like Jefferson County in Texas, where the jury verdicts tend to be higher. They put what county you're in into that spreadsheet.

They put what other types of damages you might have. Do you have permanent scarring or disfigurement, physical impairment, lost wages, mental anguish? Things like that they can legitimately justify. Mental anguish – just because you have an accident, doesn't entitle you to it. You've got to have a severe, severe situation and typically be in need of psychiatric or psychological counseling.

If you witness your family in a vehicle catching fire and exploding and burning alive, you're going to have mental anguish. If you just have an average ordinary fender-bender, you're not likely to have mental anguish. It just depends on that set of facts, and they'll put that in there.

Here's what's directly responsive to your question: on that same formula they add, "Do they have a lawyer, and if so, who? "What those insurance companies do is they go by bar card numbers. They look up those lawyers. They know which lawyers are capable of litigating, which lawyers are capable of trying the case; who wins, who loses, who doesn't ever file a lawsuit. Who your lawyer is can directly impact the value of the offer that you get. All of those things are plugged into their computer systems, and then the computer sets out typically a low, a mid, and a high range.

What that low, mid and high stand for is what the insurance company believes their risk is. They also have in there whether or not they can pin any of the liability on you. Are you ten percent liable? Did you contribute to the negligence? Had you stopped instead of continued going, would you have avoided the accident? They look to see if they can place any fault on you, because they will lower their offer by that percentage.

The low, the mid, and the high are basically based upon what they believe their exposure is in a courtroom. They're never going to pay you more than what they think their worst day in a courtroom is because it wouldn't make good business sense. Why would they? If they believe that the worst thing that could happen to them is a jury verdict of X, they're never going to offer you more than X. That would be the high on that grid. The mid is somewhere in the middle, and the low is what they think their best day is – if you win.

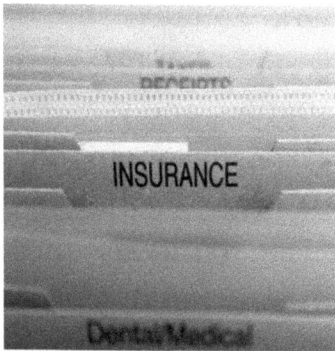

They try to offer you somewhere between the low and the mid, and a good lawyer will settle between the mid and the high, or they will get to the high.

It's rare that they're going to give you that high number, because if that is all they believe their risk is, then they're not saving any money. Insurance companies are businesses. They would rather roll the dice and see if they can save the money. They know that the high rarely happens.

The fair place for settlement is somewhere between that mid and that high mark. You take the lawyer out of that equation, and it drastically lowers those numbers on those insurance algorithms. That's another important reason to hire not just any personal injury lawyer, but a personal injury lawyer with a reputation for trying cases and winning them. Just by having their name associated with your case, the amount of money you're going to get offered typically will increase.

WHAT TO LOOK FOR WHEN RETAINING THE SERVICES OF AN ATTORNEY

Interviewer: What would you do if you were in an accident? How would you know, when you interview attorneys, who's good and who's not? What would you look for?

Ryan Bormaster: I would do my research. I would first see how easy it is to get in touch with their people, their staff, their office. How willing are they to take my calls? How responsive are they to my questions? I would see how difficult it is to have a face-to-face meeting with the guy. I would look them up on the Internet and see what I could find.

"A GOOD LAWYER KNOWS THE LAW. A GREAT LAWYER KNOWS THE JUDGE".

If someone looks me up, they're going to find that here in 2014; I was rated by Super Lawyers under their Rising Star category. That's very, very rare to get. The way that works is it's not something you can buy your way into. You can't pay to advertise with them to get it. You have to be nominated by enough of your colleagues in the legal community in Texas to even get on their radar.

There are committees that look at what you do. There's a committee of past Super Lawyers at the top. There's a committee of people that look into your professional and personal background. They talk to judges, opposing attorneys, people you've deposed, and they score you. They look into your educational background, your personal life, where you grew up, the kind of person you were – and they score you.

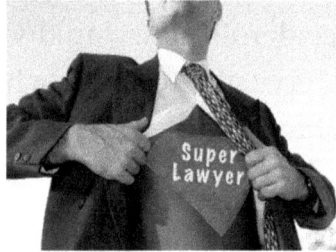

You have to be in the top five percent of those scores to make Super Lawyers, and the top 2.7 percent of that five percent to make Rising Stars. I had the honor of being inducted into Rising Stars in 2014. I will be in "Texas Monthly" magazine in April, and I'm already on the Super Lawyers website. You can see that designation on my website and click on the link to read all about it.

I would look for people that have been recognized, not just on their own website stating their own victories, but by their peers. I think that if you do your own research and you see and make sure that you feel comfortable with them, you're going to find the right fit.

Interviewer: Any other signals or signs besides the Super Lawyers? Maybe any other accolades – Better Business Bureau, or other things like that?

Ryan Bormaster: Anybody can pay a fee to get listed with the Better Business Bureau. To stay with them, you have to avoid having people file complaints against you. Certainly they're a good measure of whether or not someone's going to have a complaint filed. There's not a whole lot that I'm aware of that they do in the legal arena.

You want to check the State Bar, and look and see if there have been grievances filed against this attorney. The State Bar of Texas has a website where you can type in an attorney's name and it'll show you their profile and whether or not they had grievances against them. Really and truly, you can ask around word of mouth. The important thing is this (you'll be able to tell this when you meet with them): you want to find a lawyer that recognizes that you didn't budget for an attorney. You're in that person's office because something went wrong, and you don't like the fact that you have to be there, but you know that it's the best alternative for you. You want someone that respects that and is going to treat you as a person, not just a number on a file.

One way you can do that is to see how responsive they are to you. If you have not even signed their contract yet and they're taking your calls on a daily basis, answering your questions, and offering to help you and to whisper in your ear, then you have found a law firm that will likely take their time and that truly cares about their clients. If they're willing to do it for you when you haven't even signed a contract and they're not making any money doing it, then that should speak volumes for what they would do for you if they did have you as a client.

Know what Questions to Ask

Interviewer: Can you give me maybe two sample things people could ask the attorney that would help them gauge if they're good or not?

Ryan Bormaster: Sure. I would ask the lawyer, number one, "What can you tell me about what my case might have a value at?" If the lawyer tells you, "You're going to get three times your medicals," or "We can get you X amount of dollars," run; run fast. No lawyer is going to be able to answer that question in a first meeting. They have to first review the accident report. They have to look and see what your medical injuries are – things that you might not even know yet because you haven't had an MRI. You might be hurt, but you don't know the extent of those injuries.

You don't know if you're going to need epidural steroid injections. You don't know if you're going to need a surgery. You don't know if you're going to have a permanent impairment rating that's going to prevent you from doing things into the future or for the rest of your life. For a lawyer to answer that question right off the cuff means that they're selling you and not genuinely responding to your question. That's one thing you can do.

The second thing that you might do is ask that lawyer, "Are you willing to take a case to trial, and how often do you do that in this area?" Lawyers that are willing to pick juries (and you can check those numbers) are typically going to bring better value to your case. If they tell you, "Yes, I take cases to trial, and yes, I am willing to go all the way to verdict," you can see that very easily by doing a search of their bar card in their local jurisdiction. You can search by name. You can go to the State Bar website to get their bar card number. You can search by name or by bar card number in the local jurisdiction, and you can see how many cases they've filed and how many cases have gone to verdict. You can see those things to help you gauge whether or not they're answering you honestly, and with integrity, or whether or not they're just trying to sell you.

Those that are willing to fight all the way to the edge – win or lose – are the ones that you know will have your back through thick or thin. Even if their track record isn't necessarily stellar in a courtroom, every time they try a case to a jury verdict, they gain more experience and have learned from that experience, more so than most of their peers. A very small percentage are willing to go all the way to a jury trial. The things that they take away and learn from those experiences help shape their advice to you, and help shape what they're going to do to represent you. That helps benefit and add value to your case.

COST & COMPENSATION

Interviewer: When you make the decision to hire, how much does an auto accident lawyer cost, and how do you guys get paid?

Ryan Bormaster: A good automobile accident lawyer is never going to charge you a penny unless they recover for you. They will frontload their case expenses. They will frontload the attorneys' fees.

They will frontload what it costs them to pay their staff and their office, and they will make sure that you are taken care of all the way down the line, without ever expecting a dime back unless they recover for you.

For example, I charge a contingent fee, which means I take a percentage of what I'm able to recover for you at the end of the day and I take back my hard expenses if I'm able to recover for you. If I can't recover for you, that's my risk, and I eat it.

Interviewer: Is there a typical percentage or range of the contingency amount?

Ryan Bormaster: It depends on whether or not you can get it settled without having to file a lawsuit, or whether or not you have to file a lawsuit. It might change again if you have to actually go to trial. What I've seen are ranges of anywhere between one-third and 45 percent. Anything higher than that is not a reasonable fee, in my opinion.

CASE TIMEFRAME

Interviewer: How long do these cases take, on average, to get to either a settlement or a trial or a resolution?

Ryan Bormaster: That depends on the facts of the case. Every case is different. If you were in a low-impact, soft tissue damage case where you just need a few weeks of conservative therapy – maybe hot packs and cold packs and massages and electric stimulation – your case is going to settle much more quickly.

If it's a longer case – if you need surgical intervention, or steroid injections or both – that case is going to take longer. On the short end, you might be looking at anywhere between three and six months, from cradle to grave. That way, you can determine that you are in fact better and that you don't leave that doctor and settle your case and then two weeks later turn the wrong way and go, "Oops, that hurt. That didn't feel right."

A good lawyer is never going to rush it. They're going to make sure that you have recovered, so that you don't find yourself in a situation where they have advised you to settle and you've taken that money, and it turns out you were in worse shape than you thought.

If you are going to have to try a case and litigate it, then you're looking typically at 18 months, on the low end, from the time you file that lawsuit, to the time you have that privilege of getting in front of a judge/jury for trial.

The reason for that is really simple. There are 25-some-odd civil judges in Harris County, for example. There are about a quarter of a million cases or more that get filed: everything from, "I was in an auto accident," to "Somebody sold me a lemon car," to "My boss was discriminating against me," to "I've got to get a divorce." They're all in front of the same judges. Typically, you're in line with everybody else from the time you file; your spot is held, but it takes that long until you have your day in court.

Lawyers need that time, because during that time is when we go to town. That's when we roll up our sleeves and go to work. We issue subpoenas, we request affidavits, and we take depositions. We do the things that are necessary to get your evidence into an admissible form and to get your case ready for trial.

In this computer age, anybody can go to the Internet, print out a bill, and make it look like it came from a hospital or a doctor. That's not admissible. You have to have some indication of reliability – typically a deposition on written questions with an affidavit from the facility. There are things that you need to do to make those records admissible and acceptable to a courtroom before you can even talk about them. We spend that time gathering those things as you're being treated and getting better and doing what we need to do in order to maximize more chances of success.

Typical Case Resolutions

Interviewer: What happens for most of the cases? Do most settle? Do most go to trial? What's typical?

Ryan Bormaster: I would say that 95, if not 98 percent of the cases I've had to file in the last 13 years have settled without having to go pick a jury. It takes time, and I've had to work over the other side. I've had to engage in depositions and discovery and make things hard on them. Eventually, they will realize their risks, reevaluate, and make you an offer. It's a much smaller percentage that you actually have to pick a jury on. I've done it many, many times over the years, but it's rare. It's rare that you have to do that.

SCENARIOS INVOLVING UNINSURED OR UNDERINSURED PEOPLE.

Interviewer: What happens if you get into an accident with someone who has no insurance or not enough insurance, or that kind of thing? Can you still recover anything from your own insurance company? What could you do?

Ryan Bormaster: That depends on if you have the right kind of insurance. I strongly suggest and recommend that people shop around. I advise that. You want to have comprehensive and collision and personal injury protection. You want to have those things. You want to have rental car coverage. You want to have everything that you would hope the other driver would have. If they don't, it is highly unlikely that you are going to get the immediate assistance that you need.

If the other driver that you hit happens to be the CEO of a Fortune 500 company, you're probably okay because they've got assets. The average ordinary Joe on the street has minimum limits coverage. In Texas, that's $30,000. If you're in a serious injury with broken bones, that is not even going to begin to cover your injuries. The only way you cover those is with comprehensive collision, uninsured/underinsured, PIP, and rental car coverage. You want to have all of those things, with the highest limits as you can.

Let me tell you, if you're a good driver, or even a bad driver, insurance companies are very competitive with that kind of stuff. Every insurance company lets you pay out your premium over six months. Even for the highest of limits, on average it's not going to cost you more than a few hundred dollars a month, if that. You're paying for peace of mind – knowing that you've got hundreds of thousands of dollars in your own coverage to protect you against the eventuality where someone either doesn't have insurance or only has minimum limits.

ASSISTANCE WITH MEDICAL BILLS

Interviewer: Are you able to help people negotiate down medical bills, or deal with Medicare or liens or problems medical-wise?

Ryan Bormaster: Absolutely. When you've got a good lawyer involved, they've got a network of quality people that will treat you without you having to come out-of-pocket up front. Those people will expect to be paid at the end of the day.

Because your lawyer has a volume of clients and because you've chosen someone that has a good reputation, and someone that you know is good at what they do, they have typically over the years developed relationships with the networks that they're involved in, such that the doctors are willing to cut you breaks. They're willing to negotiate down their bills after settlement, so that you can be made whole.

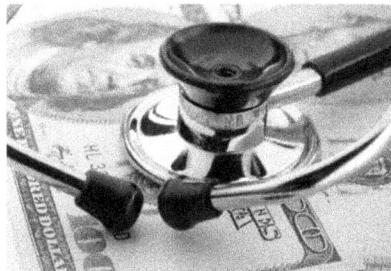

Let's say, for example, you've got $50,000 in medical bills and a $30,000 policy. Often times, a lawyer will be able to turn that $50,000 maybe into $15,000 or even $10,000.It would blow your mind, the type of negotiations and the type of reductions that lawyers can get – not because the doctor wants to charge that, not because their services weren't worth more, but because a) they know they're getting more business from that lawyer in the future, and b) more importantly, good lawyers surround themselves with doctors who are empathic, and they care. They have empathy for their patients, and they don't want to put them into bankruptcy. They want them to be made whole. They're more willing when they know they're working with a straight-up lawyer who's reputable, to take that leap of faith and trust that when a lawyer says, "I need this kind of reduction," they need to give it on that particular case.

ADVICE FOR AUTO ACCIDENT SCENES

Interviewer: Do you have any suggestions for people that are at the scene, things they can do? If they take pictures and document the scene, can that be used as evidence?

Ryan Bormaster: Absolutely, I've got suggestions. The first suggestion I have is that that person, if they're reading this book, should go to my website and call me. I have an accident survival guide that's the shape and size of a credit card. It's an accordion that fits in your wallet. Its two magnets the size of credit cards that have paper in between them. It'll fit in your wallet with your other credit cards. You can open that up if you're ever in an accident and you don't even have to think about it because it takes you step by step with what you need to do and document at the scene of that accident. You can come bring it into me and trade it out for a new one.

That being said, for those of you that don't take the time to call me or go to my website, you need to remember to record everything. If you're able to take pictures, take pictures. If you're able to record the other driver admitting fault by apologizing to you, record them. Texas is a one-party consent state. What that means is that only one of the two people on the recording has to know

and consent to that recording. It can even be the person doing the recording.

If you have an accident in Texas, you can turn on your video recorder or your audio recorder on your I-Phone or smartphone, and just start picking up everything so that you can catch the other guy. You want to record it all. You want to take pictures. You want to document. You want to tell the officer that you are hurt. If you don't tell them you are hurt, they're going to put "no injury" on the accident report. If you tell them you're hurt, they're going to put, "possible injury." You want to make sure that you give statements, and that you get the names and phone numbers of witnesses. You want to get their statements. If they saw you and they can corroborate your story and they can help you, then that can be very important.

I can't tell you how many times I've crossed the bridge to people that have said, "He told me this at the scene," and all of a sudden, when the insurance adjustor called, it's a completely different story.

WORKING WITH ATTORNEYS

Interviewer: When someone's been in an accident and they're interviewing lawyers, and maybe they've even started working with one, what can people do on their side to help the lawyer help them to have a better case and a better outcome?

Ryan Bormaster: They can follow their lawyer's advice. They can make sure that they make every doctor's appointment, even if they don't feel like going. They can make sure that they get full and detailed information; don't leave anything out. The lawyer will decide whether or not it's important. They need to bring in with them their pictures and the things that they did to document the accident at the scene. If it's somebody that went to my website, bring me that accident survival guide.

Those are the things that they can do to help maximize their case. They need to call their lawyers back when their lawyers' offices call them. They need to call their doctors back when their doctors' offices call them. They need to make time to get the testing and the treatment and the things that will a) make them feel better, which is the most important, and b) add value to their case.

DISCLAIMER

This publication is intended to be informational only. No legal advice is being given, and no attorney-client relationship is intended to be created by reading this material. If you are facing legal issues, whether criminal or civil, seek professional legal counsel to get your questions answered.

R.B. BORMASTER & ASSOCIATES, P.C.

2425 Fountain View
Ste 290
Houston, TX 77057
(713) 714-4000

www.BormasterLaw.com